Arthur Wentworth Hamilton Eaton

Acadian Legends and Lyrics

Arthur Wentworth Hamilton Eaton

Acadian Legends and Lyrics

ISBN/EAN: 9783744652056

Printed in Europe, USA, Canada, Australia, Japan

Cover: Foto ©Thomas Meinert / pixelio.de

More available books at **www.hansebooks.com**

Acadian Legends and Lyrics

By
ARTHUR WENTWORTH EATON

LONDON AND NEW YORK
WHITE & ALLEN
MDCCLXXXIX

I INSCRIBE HERE

TWO NAMES THAT LIVE TOGETHER

IN MY LOVE

ANNA AUGUSTA WILLOUGHBY

HAMILTON EATON

AND

SUSAN HAMILTON

The vaulted chambers of the poet's brain
    Are peopled by a restless throng who beat
    Bewildering music, sometimes low and sweet,
Sometimes a loud, wild-resonant refrain.

There glide soft-sheeted ghosts of long spent years,—
    Sweet, sensuous loves of youth that lived an hour,
    Hope's phantom forms, delicious dreams of power,
When all the world was new, and later fears

Entangled not the boy's swift-flying feet.
    Beneath the dim, unearthly arches hide
    Odors from far-off flowers, and there abide
The mother-songs that childhood's ears first greet.

CONTENTS.

ACADIAN LEGENDS :—
                                                                            PAGE

The Naming of the Gaspereau	3
L'Ordre de Bon Temps	8
The Legend of Glooscap	11
Departure of Glooscap	15
Resettlement of Acadia	19
L'Ile Sainte Croix	25
Phantom Light of the Baie des Chaleurs	28
Marguerite and the Isle of Demons	31
De Soto's Last Dream	36
The Jubilee of Acadia College	41

LYRICS :—

Charles River, by the Bridge	47
The Whaling Town	51
Flood Tide	53
I Watch the Ships	55
Foundry Fires	58
The Old New England Meeting House	60
At Grandmother's	63
Children of the Sun	66

CONTENTS.

Fairy Folk	68
The Street Organ	71
The Angel Sleep	72
The Roots of the Roses	74
Chance Meetings	75
The Poet Passed My Way	77
The Voyage of Sleep	78
Gems That Are Rarest	80
La Douleur du Peintre	81
Sometime	84
'Twere Better to Love	86
The Hearth is Cold	87
After Separation	88
I Plucked a Daisy	89
The Meadow Lands	91
Small and Great	92
Life	93
It Matters Much	94
Not in Vain	96
To a Doubter	98
The Suicide	100
An Answer	102
Despondency	104
A Fire of Straw	105
Reabsorption into Deity	106
Eder's Watchtower	109
Day of the Triumphant Sun	112

CONTENTS.

My Purest Longings Spring . . . 115
Brotherhood 117
The Ancient Gods are Dead . . . 119
O Easter Queen 121
Fountains Abbey 123
To Lord Hamilton of Dalzell . . . 128

SONNETS:—

O Restless Poet Soul . . . 135
The Awakening 136
Love's Slavery 137
Separation 138
Pain 139
Love Letters 140
The Virgin's Shrine 141
If Christ were Here 142
A Dream of Christ. No. I. . . . 143
" " No. II. . . . 144
Deepening the Channel 145
Matthew Arnold 146
Elisha Mulford 147
Harvard Commencement 148

ACADIAN LEGENDS.

THE NAMING OF THE GASPEREAU.

ABOUT 1673.

NOW the rainbow tints of autumn
   Deck the ancient hills
And the dreamy river saunters
   Past the lazy mills,
Let us seek the murmuring forest
   Where the pines and hemlocks grow
And a thousand fringéd shadows
   Fall upon the Gaspereau.

When the old Acadian farmers,
   Sailing up the Bay,
Landed with their goods and cattle
   On the fair Grand Pré,
Wandering through the ancient forest
   Claude, René, and Theriot,
In a vale of matchless beauty
   Found the River Gaspereau.

Found the lithe and dark-skinned Micmac,
    In his birch canoe,
Paddling down his *Magapskegechk*
    To the Basin blue,
Little dreaming of the presence
    Of the Indian's pale-faced foe
Singing unmelodious boat-songs
    On the winding Gaspereau.

Midst the brushwood and the rushes
    And the trembling ferns,
Where the River, sighing, singing,
    Speeds with many turns
Through the gateway of the mountains
    Toward the meadows far below,
On they crept in silent wonder
    By the sun-kissed Gaspereau.

These were days of dream and legend,
    Continents were new,
Here the humble Norman peasants
    Into poets grew;
From their roaming in the forest
    Claude, René, and Theriot

Brought their comrades rapt descriptions
   Of the vale of Gaspereau.

Then around the hemlock fire,
   In the cabin rude,
With their stock of cheese and brown-bread
   And their ale, home-brewed,
Gathered all the Norman peasants;
   And at last René said low:
" Let us name the new-found river
   Gaspére-water, Gaspereau ! "

Gaspére was the gentlest comrade
   In their little band,
None so buoyant, none so eager
   For the Acadian land;
But ere half the voyage was over,
   In the wastes of summer seas,
Suddenly there crept beside him
   Some old shadow of disease.

There was mourning in the vessel,
   Strong men sobbed and cried,
When one evening, just at sunset,
   Their loved Gaspére died ;

There was wailing in the vessel
   As, with trembling voice and slow,
Pere Deschambault read the death-prayers
   As the still form sank below.

Dreary seemed the voyage thereafter
   On the cruel sea,
Till they reached the smiling meadows
   Of fair Acadie.
Never rose their songs at evening,
   For the flame of hope burned low;—
So they named the lovely river,
   With fond memory, Gaspereau!

Thence, in summer, when the plowing
   In the fields was done,
And the busy looms were growing
   Silent, one by one,
Many a lover in the moonlight,
   Speaking tender words and low,
Sought the path across the meadows
   To the quiet Gaspereau.

When there came some loss or sorrow
   To the little band;

When the dykes broke, or the crops failed
   In the Acadian land,
Many a tired wife and mother,
   All her spirit dark with woe,
Sought relief from her forebodings
   By the peaceful Gaspereau.

Vanished are the Acadian peasants,
   Sweet Evangeline,
Gabriel, Benedict, and Basil,
   And no sadder scene
Ever gave itself to story,
   Than that scene of wreck and woe,
When the English ships weighed anchor
   In the mouth of Gaspereau.

Still it flows among the meadows,
   Singing as of yore
To the ferns and trailing mosses
   On the winding shore;
To the pines that dip their branches
   In the crystal wave below,
And the crimson leaves of autumn
   Falling in the Gaspereau.

L'ORDRE DE BON TEMPS.

TWO hundred years ago and more
   In History's romance,
The white flag of the Bourbons flew
   From all the gates of France.

And even on these wild Western shores
   Rock-clad and forest-mailed,
The Bourbon name, King Henry's fame
   With "Vive le Roi" was hailed.

O "Vive le Roi!" and "Vive le Roi!"
   Those wild adventurous days
When brave Champlain and Poutrincourt
   Explored the Acadian bays.

When from Port Royal's rude-built walls
   Gleamed o'er the hills afar
The golden lilies of the shield
   Of Henry of Navarre.

A gay and gallant company
   Those voyagers of old
Whose life in the Acadian fort
   Lescarbot's verse has told.

Their "Order of Good Times" was formed
   For mirth and mutual cheer;
And many a tale and many a song
   Beguiled that winter drear.

Aye, while the snow lay softly o'er
   The meadows crisp and bare,
And hooded all the clustering hills
   Like nuns of Saint-Hilaire,

Each day they spread a goodly feast
   Not anywise too poor
For cafés of the nobles in
   The famous Rue Aux Ours.

And as the old French clock rang out,
   With echoes musical,
Twelve silvery strokes, the hour of noon,
   Through the pine-scented hall,

The Master of the Order came
    To serve each hungry guest,
A napkin o'er his shoulder thrown,
    And flashing on his breast,

A collar decked with diamonds,
    Fair pearls, turquoises blue;
While close behind in warrior dress
    Walked old chief Membertou.

Then wine went round and friends were pledged,
    With gracious courtesy,
And ne'er was heard one longing word
    For France beyond the sea.

O days of bold adventure past;
    O gay, adventurous men,
Your "Order of Good Times" I think
    Shall ne'er be seen again!

THE LEGEND OF GLOOSCAP.

BARING its breast to the sun as of yore
Lieth the peaceful Acadian shore;
Fertile and fair, in the dew and the rain,
Ripen its fields of golden grain.

Like a sabred sentinel grim and gray
Blomidon stands at the head of the Bay,
And the famous Fundy tides at will
Sweep into Minas Basin still.

From its home in the hills the Gaspereau
Sings as it strays to the sea below,
Wanders on till it wakes in the tide
A muddy river, deep and wide.

Here at the edge of the ancient wood
Is the spot where Basil's smithy stood;
Close to these clustering willows green
Was the home of his love, Evangeline.

This is the old Acadian shore
Prized by the poet more and more
As he lives in the loves and hopes, and hears
Silvery strains from the silent years.

Long ere the Frenchmen drove away
The cruel tides from the fair Grand Pré,
And bound the dykes like emerald bands
Round the Acadian meadow lands,

The Micmac sailed in his birch canoe
Over the Basin calm and blue,
With salmon spear to the lakeside crept,
Then by his wigwam fire slept.

Far in the depths of the forest gray
Hunted the moose the livelong day;
While the Micmac mother crooned to her child
Forest folk-songs weird and wild.

Over the tribe with jealous eye
Watched the Great Spirit from on high;
In the purple mists of Blomidon
The god-man, Glooscap, had his throne.

No matter how far his feet might stray
From the favorite haunts of his tribe away,
The Micmac's cry of faith or fear
Failed not to find his Glooscap's ear.

'Twas he who had made for the Indian's use
Beaver and bear, and sent the moose
Roaming over the wild woodlands;
He who had strewn upon the sands

Of the tide-swept shore of the stormy bay
Amethysts purple, and agates gray;
And into the heart of love had flung
That which keeps love ever young.

Then the Frenchmen came, a thrifty band,
Who felled the forest and sowed the land,
And drove from their haunts by the sunny shore
Micmac and moose forevermore.

And Glooscap, the god-man, sore distrest,
Hid himself in the unknown West,
And the Micmac kindled his wigwam fire
Far from the grave of his child and his sire,

Where now as he weaves his basket gay,
And paddles his birch canoe away,
He dreams of the happy time for men
When Glooscap shall come to his tribe again.

THE DEPARTURE OF GLOOSCAP.

LONG ago before the Frenchman
    Stemmed the mighty tides of Fundy,
Steered his bark to Minas Basin,
    Blue and peaceful as to-day;
Long before the workman's hammer
Rang its busy strokes at morning
On the rude walls of the cabin
    Rising near the fair Grand Pré,

Glooscap left his loving subjects,
Bade farewell to Megumaage,
Holding first a parting banquet
    On the Minas Basin shore;
Thither came the wolves and beavers,
Came the martens and the foxes
And the white owls and the turtles
    And the loons and many more.

And they feasted long, but sadly,
Till a gleam of silver moonlight,

Shooting o'er the silent water,
    Lighted frowning Blomidon.
Then uprose the mighty Glooscap,
Left the feast, and moving swiftly
As the West Wind when it travels
    Through the giant pines alone,

Bade the tide return to seaward,
Pushed his great canoe upon it,
Glided off upon the Basin,
    Singing sadly as he went;
And the people of the forest,
All the wolves and bears and beavers,
Listening to the song of Glooscap,
    Gazed in silent wonderment.

Till his voice grew faint and fainter,
And the water of the Basin
Rippling in the silver moonlight
    Was the only sound they heard.
Then the wolves and bears and beavers,
Who till now had all been brothers,
Lost the gift of common language,
    And no longer beast and bird

Lived in peace in Megumaage,
But with hatred of each other
Fled into the darkest forest
    Where the wild *menichkul* grow,
And the great white-owl in anguish
Wailed " koo-koo-shoes " ! I am sorry,
And the loons beloved of Glooscap
    Uttered strange, wild notes of woe.

There was wailing in the forest,
There were sobs among the pine boughs,
Lamentations deep and dreadful
    From the oak trees on the hills;
All the flowers with choking voices
Told their sorrow to each other,
Mournful sang Seboo, the river,
    And the little laughing rills.

For they knew at last was over
All the happy reign of Glooscap,
Whose right hand had taught the Micmac
    All the useful arts he knew,
Whose fierce bow had slain the giant,
Killed Chenoo the icy-hearted,

And the great Wind-Bird, Wuchowsen,
    And the terrible Culloo.

So he left them, mighty Glooscap,
And they tell us he is making
Arrows in his lofty wigwam
    Far beyond the setting sun,
Arrows of the birch and poplar
For some dreadful day of battle,
When the Micmac's foes shall perish
    And his wanderings be done.

And they tell us some have found him,
After seven years of seeking,
In the forests of the sunset
    Where there dwell no Micmac men;
They have feasted in his wigwam,
Where he lives in peace and plenty,
And have heard his faithful promise
    That he shall return again.

THE RESETTLEMENT OF ACADIA.

THE rocky slopes for emerald had changed their garb of gray
When the vessels from Connecticut came sailing up the Bay;
There were diamonds on every wave that drew the strangers on,
And wreaths of wild arbutus round the brows of Blomidon.

Five years in desolation the Acadian land had lain,
Five golden harvest moons had wooed the fallow fields in vain,
Five times the winter snows caressed, and summer sunsets smiled
On lonely clumps of willows, and fruit trees growing wild.

There was silence in the forest and along the Minas shore,
And not a habitation from Canard to Beau Séjour,

But many a ruined cellar, and many a broken wall,
Told the story of Acadia's prosperity and fall.

And even in the sunshine of that peaceful day in June,
When Nature swept her harp and found her strings in perfect tune,
The land seemed calling wildly for its owners far away,
The exiles scattered on the coast, from Maine to Charleston Bay;

Where with many bitter longings for their fair homes and their dead,
They bowed their heads in anguish and would not be comforted;
And like the Jewish exiles, long ago, beyond the sea,
They could not sing the songs of home, in their captivity.

But the simple Norman peasant-folk shall till the land no more,
For the vessels from Connecticut have anchored by the shore,
And many a sturdy Puritan, his mind with Scripture stored,
Rejoices he has found at last, "the garden of the Lord."

There are families from Tolland, from Killingworth
    and Lyme,
Gentle mothers, tender maidens, and strong men in
    their prime,
There are lovers who have plighted their vows in
    Coventry,
And merry children dancing o'er the vessels' decks in
    glee.

They come as came the Hebrews into their promised
    land,
Not as to wild New England's shores came first the
    Pilgrim band;
The Minas fields were fruitful, and the Gaspereau had
    borne
To seaward many a vessel with its freight of yellow
    corn.

They come with hearts as true as are their manners
    blunt and cold
To found a race of noblemen of stern New England
    mould,
A race of earnest people whom the coming years shall
    teach

The broader ways of knowledge, and the gentler forms
    of speech.

They come as Puritans, but who shall say their hearts
    are blind
To the subtle charms of nature, and the love of human-
    kind ?
The blue laws of Connecticut have shaped their
    thought, tis true,
But human laws can never wholly Heaven's work undo.

And tears fall fast from many an eye, long time unused
    to weep,
For o'er the fields lay whitening the bones of cows and
    sheep,
The faithful cows that used to feed upon the broad
    Grand Pré,
And with their tinkling bells come slowly home at close
    of day.

And where the Acadian village stood, its roofs o'er-
    grown with moss,
And the simple wooden chapel, with its altar and its
    cross,

And where the forge of Basil sent its sparks toward the sky,
The lonely thistle blossomed, and the fire weed grew high.

* * * * * * * *

The broken dykes have been rebuilt, a century and more,
The cornfields stretch their furrows from Canard to Beau Séjour,
Five generations have been reared beside the fair Grand Pré,
Since the vessels from Connecticut came sailing up the Bay.

And now across the meadows, while the farmers reap and sow,
The engine shrieks its discords to the hills of Gaspereau,
And ever onward to the sea the restless Fundy tide
Bears playful pleasure yachts and busy trade ships, side by side.

And the Puritan has yielded to the softening touch of time,

Like him who still content remained in Killingworth
    and Lyme,
And graceful homes of prosperous men make all the
    landscape fair,
And mellow creeds and ways of life are rooted every-
    where.

And churches nestle lovingly on many a glad hill-side,
And holy bells rings out their music in the eventide;
But here and there on untilled ground, apart from glebe
    or town,
Some lone, surviving apple tree stands leafless, bare,
    and brown.

And many a traveller has found, as thoughtlessly he
    strayed,
Some long-forgotten cellar in the deepest thicket's
    shade,
And clumps of willows by the dykes, sweet scented,
    fair, and green,
That seemed to tell again the story of Evangeline.

L'ILE SAINTE CROIX.

[Where the first French settlement in America was made.]

WITH tangled brushwood all o'ergrown,
    And here and there a lofty pine,
    Around whose form strange creepers twine,
And crags that mock the wild sea's moan;

And little bays where no ships come,
    Though many a white sail passes by,
    And many a white cloud in the sky
Looks down and shames the sleeping foam,

Unconscious on the waves it lies,
    While, midst the golden reeds and sedge
    That, southward, line the water's edge,
The thrush sings her shrill melodies.

No human dwelling now is seen
    Upon its rude, unfertile slopes,
    Though many a summer traveller gropes
For ruins midst the tangled green;

And seeks upon the northern shore
   The graves of the adventurous band
   That followed to this western land
Champlain, De Monts, and Poutrincourt.

There stood the ancient fort that sent
   Fierce cannon echoes through the wold,
   There waved the Bourbon flag that told
The mastery of a continent.

There through the pines the echoing wail
   Of ghostly winds was heard at eve,
   And hoarse, deep sounds like those that heave
The breasts of stricken warriors pale.

There Huguenots and cassocked priests,
   And noble-born and sons of toil,
   Together worked the barren soil,
And shared each other's frugal feasts.

And heard across the sailless sea
   A strange, prophetic harvest tune,
   And saw beneath the yellow moon
The golden reapings that should be.

Till stealthy winter through the reeds
    Crept, crystal-footed, to the shore,
    And to the little hamlet bore
His hidden freight of deadly seeds.

Spring came at last, and o'er the waves
    The welcome sail of Pontgravé;
    But half the number silent lay,
Death's pale first-fruits, in western graves.

Sing on, wild sea, your sad refrain,
    For all the gallant sons of France,
    Whose songs and sufferings enhance
The romance of the western main.

Sing requiems to these tangled woods,
    With ruined forts and hidden graves;
    Your mournful music history craves
For many of her noblest moods.

THE PHANTOM LIGHT OF THE BAIE DES CHALEURS.

'TIS the laughter of pines that swing and sway
  Where the breeze from the land meets the breeze from the bay,
'Tis the silvery foam of the silver tide
In ripples that reach to the forest side;
'Tis the fisherman's boat, in a track of sheen
Plying through tangled seaweed green,
  O'er the Baie des Chaleurs.

Who has not heard of the phantom light
That over the moaning waves, at night,
Dances and drifts in endless play,
Close to the shore, then far away,
Fierce as the flame in sunset skies,
Cold as the winter light that lies
  On the Baie des Chaleurs.

They tell us that many a year ago,
From lands where the palm and the olive grow,

Where vines with their purple clusters creep
Over the hillsides gray and steep,
A knight in his doublet, slashed with gold,
Famed, in that chivalrous time of old,
For valorous deeds and courage rare,
Sailed with a princess wondrous fair
      To the Baie des Chaleurs.

That a pirate crew from some isle of the sea,
A murderous band as e'er could be,
With a shadowy sail, and a flag of night,
That flaunted and flew in heaven's sight,
Sailed in the wake of the lovers there,
And sank the ship and its freight so fair
      In the Baie des Chaleurs.

Strange is the tale that the fishermen tell;
They say that a ball of fire fell
Straight from the sky, with crash and roar,
Lighting the bay from shore to shore;
Then the ship, with shudder and with groan,
Sank through the waves to the caverns lone
      Of the Baie des Chaleurs.

That was the last of the pirate crew;
But many a night a black flag flew
From the mast of a spectre vessel, sailed
By a spectre band that wept and wailed
For the wreck they had wrought on the sea, on the land,
For the innocent blood they had spilt on the sand
      Of the Baie des Chaleurs.

This is the tale of the phantom light
That fills the mariner's heart, at night,
With dread as it gleams o'er his path on the bay,
Now by the shore, then far away,
Fierce as the flame in sunset skies,
Cold as the winter moon that lies
      On the Baie des Chaleurs.

MARGUERITE AND THE ISLE OF DEMONS.

P AST the coral reefs and islands
    In blue, palm-fringed Southern seas,
Toward the great St. Lawrence, gaily
    Sped a French ship in the breeze.
Bearing northward priests and nobles,
    High-born women, soldiers tall,
Midst them, ever stern and gloomy,
    The proud viceroy, Roberval.

Many a day, dark-browed and silent,
    He the men and maids would meet
On the vessel's deck, and always
    Toward his niece, fair Marguerite,
Send fierce glances, as when storm-clouds
    Shoot into the tropic sky,
Driving bright-winged birds for shelter
    To the mango-forests high.

And the haughty women gave her
    Looks of pity or of scorn,

For her troth had long been plighted
   To a lover, humbly-born,
Brave, but wild and pleasure-loving
   As the young stag on the moor,
Seeking now some new adventure
   On this romance-breathing shore.

Ever northward sailed the vessel
   Many and many an ocean mile,
Toward the mouth of the St. Lawrence
   And the blue straits of Belleisle,
Where to lonely shores and islands
   Silver sea-birds come in flocks,
And the white surf, fiercely foaming,
   Breaks upon the sullen rocks.

Suddenly the Isle of Demons,
   Hardly half a league away,
Loomed before them, and the Viceroy
   Sternly called: "Come here, I pray."
And his niece obeyed, and trembling
   Stood before him near the rail,
And the other maidens, watching,
   Saw her face grow deathly pale.

Not a word he spoke, but only,
   With that fierce light in his eye,
Pointed to the Isle of Demons;
   Then he turned, and presently
Came the white-sailed ship to anchor,
   And above the wild surf's roar
Marguerite heard mocking voices:
   "Dwell with us forevermore!"

As the mother soothes her baby,
   When its cry grows worse and worse,
Now, with loving looks, hung o'er her
   Old Marie, her Norman nurse,
And her tears fell with the maiden's,
   As she sobbed "Ma belle petite,
Old Marie will share the exile
   Of her little Marguerite."

Then the women wept and pleaded
   With the Viceroy, Roberval,
And the men, but he unyielding,
   Gave no heed to them at all;
And they watched her as the rowers
   Bore her up the distant bay,

While the ship lay fast at anchor
    Almost half a league away.

How the demons pressed about her;
    How they mocked her woman's woe;
From the gray cliffs rang their laughter
    To the echoing caves below.
How she saw the flowers tremble
    Where they danced with death-shod feet,
Heard their jarring voices call her:
    "Marguerite, O, Marguerite!"

Then they gathered closer round her,
    Great and small, to do her harm;
But the Virgin-Mother sheltered
    Marguerite with her right-arm;
And she fought them, and grew stronger
    Ever as she knelt to pray,
Till at last the demons, shrieking,
    Fled into the woods away.

And ere long she grew so holy,
    That they shunned her in affright,
Never spoke her name save only

On the distant cliffs at night.
So she lived three lonely summers,
   Longing for some happy chance,
That might give her back her lover,
   On the sunny shores of France.

Till a little fishing vessel
   From some port beyond the sea,
Drifting near the Isle of Demons,
   Gave the maid her liberty,
And the good queen and the nobles
   Hastened her return to greet,
And her faithful lover welcomed
   To his heart his Marguerite.

DE SOTO'S LAST DREAM.

ON a shadowy plain where cypress groves
    And spreading palm trees rise,
And the antlered deer, swift-footed, roves,
    The brave De Soto lies.

They have made him a bed, where overhead
    The trailing moss entwines
With the leaves of the campion flower red
    And gleaming ivy vines.

Over his fevered forehead creeps,
    From the cedar branches high,
The wind that sleeps in the liquid deeps
    Of the changeless southern sky.

And the Mississippi's turbid tide,
    Broad and free, flows past,
Like the current wide, on which men glide
    To another ocean vast.

DE SOTO'S LAST DREAM.

He dreams of the days in sunny Spain
    When heart and hope were strong,
And he hears again, on the trackless main,
    The sound of the sailor's song.

Now, with the fierce Pizarro's band,
    To wield the sword anew,
He takes command on the golden sand
    Of the shores of proud Peru.

And northward now, from Tampa Bay,
    With glittering spear and lance,
With pennons gay, and horses' neigh,
    His cohorts brave advance.

Again, as the glittering dawn awakes
    From its dreams of purple mist,
By the stoléd priests he kneels and takes
    The holy eucharist.

And the echoing woods and boundless skies
    Are hushed to soft content,
As the strains of the old Te Deum rise
    On a new continent.

Again he sees in the thicket damp,
   By the light of a ghastly moon,
The crocodile, foul from his native swamp,
   Plunge in the dark lagoon.

Again, o'er the wild savannas flee,
   From his feet, the frightened deer,
And the curlews scream, from tree to tree,
   Their strange, wild notes of fear.

Over the rich magnolia blooms
   Floats, 'neath the evening skies,
Drunk with their soft and sweet perfumes,
   The bird of paradise.

The wild macaw, on her silken nest,
   Midst the orange blossoms white,
From her scarlet breast and golden crest,
   Flashes the noon-day light.

In the waving grass, on the yucca spires,
   Flowers of pallid hue
Blend with erythrina's fires,
   And the starry nixia's blue.

DE SOTO'S LAST DREAM.

The rich gordonia blossom swells
   Where the brooklet ripples by,
And the silvery white halesia bells
   Reflect the cloudless sky.

And southern mosses, soft and brown,
   With gleaming ivies twine,
And heavy purple blooms weigh down
   The wild wistaria vine.

Now on his bold Castilian band
   The native warriors press,
From their haunts in the trackless prairie land,
   And the unknown wilderness;

And the flame he has kindled gleams again
   On his sword of trusty steel,
As he burns, midst the yells of savage men,
   Their village of Mobile.

    *   *   *   *   *   *

Like the look of triumph o'er victories won
   That dying conquerors wore,
Or the light that bursts from the setting sun
   On some wild, rugged shore,

The fire of hope lights up anew
    The brave adventurer's brow,
A roseate flash, then death's dull hue,
    And his dream is over now.

So, on the plain where cypress groves
    And spreading palm trees rise,
And the antlered deer, swift-footed, roves,
    The brave De Soto dies.

THE JUBILEE OF ACADIA COLLEGE,
AUGUST 28, 1888.

O MOTHER of our manhood days,
   Proud sons of thine are we,
As here, from all our scattered ways,
   We keep thy Jubilee.

Before us lie in purple mist
   The meadows of Grand Pré,
Thy slopes with hallow memories kissed
   Are fairer far than they.

Across the fields of golden corn
   Faint shadows come and go,
No cloud hangs o'er thy harvest morn,
   Or dims thy sunlight glow.

To thee all laurelled deeds we bring
   Our hearts or hands have done,
Here at thy feet the first buds fling
   Of worthier works begun.

Weep'st thou thy elder sons? We own,
   So pure their memories shine,
The brightest jewels in thy crown
   Are those first sons of thine.

Patient they wrought with toil and prayer,
   Ere fell the twilight gray;
In worlds unseen may they not share
   This joy of ours to-day?

The riper years from which we wring
   Wide creeds and wider cares,
Are ripe indeed if they but bring
   Devotion such as theirs.

From out these halls where first we learned
   The power of thought to know,
Where first our restless being burned
   With intellectual glow,

New sons of thine are going still;
   O mother, may they be
Men to whom Time may safely will
   An untried century.

In spheres where scattered rays of good,
    Like wandering stars shall meet,
Glad worlds, wherein the brotherhood
    Of man shall be complete,

Set thou their steps, nor let them pause
    Till thought's sweet chimes be rung
From every hill, and Nature's laws
    By every soul be sung.

So the strong sceptre of the years
    Thy woman's hand shall wield,
While ancient error disappears,
    And ancient wrongs are healed.

O mother of our manhood days,
    Proud sons of thine are we,
As here from all our scattered ways
    We keep thy Jubilee.

LYRICS.

CHARLES RIVER, BY THE BRIDGE.

WITH finest mimicry of wave and tide,
    Of ocean storm and current setting free,
Here by the bridge the river deep and wide,
Lashing the reeds along its muddy marge,
Speeds to the wharf the dusky coaling barge,
    And dreams itself a commerce-quickening sea.

East lies the city, clustering its cold spires
    Against a cloudless sky, one gilded dome
Seen everywhere, as if a hundred fires
Held jubilee upon the ancient height
Where once a solitary beacon light,
    In peace unkindled, guarded freedom's home.

Unlovely meadows westward meet the eye,
    Brown, silty, sere, where driftwood from the mills
Is thrown, as Spring's full flood sweeps by,
And weeds grow rank as on the wild sea-marsh,
And lonely cries of sea-gulls loud and harsh,
    Pierce evening's silence to the distant hills.

The scene with all its varied, subtle moods,
   My eyes have looked upon so many years,
That like my mother's songs, or the old woods
In whose mysterious shade I used to play,
Dreaming fair child-dreams in the soft noonday,
   It has strange power to waken joy or tears.

I love the lights upon the farther shore,
   That thicken, as adds silent year to year,
Long rows of gleaming lamps that more and more
Remind me of the dear souls gone, not set
Among cold jewels in God's coronet,
   But radiant still with life and hope and cheer.

Sometimes inverted in the wave they seem
   Like Bagdad's palaces and spires aflame
With jewels, or the golden towers that gleam
Amidst the visions of the holy seer
Who by the blue Ægean calm and clear,
   Saw things too fair for human lips to name.

Sometimes when all the river lies in mist,
   So far away those twinkling eyes of flame,
They seem like memories that still subsist

And glimmer faintly through the shrouded years,
Through noise and silence, laughter, cries, and tears,
  Of that white world from which our spirits came.

I cannot watch unmoved the sunset here,
  When swift, volcanic fires of purest gold
Along the hills of purple mist appear,
And clouds deep-crimsoned in the day's decline
Like fairest bridal-garments splashed with wine,
  Lie careless, resting fleecy fold on fold.

I have no words to shape the things I find
  Told in this glory of the western sky;
The best thought does not often reach the mind
Until its splendor has swept o'er the heart
In waves of feeling. Truth's sublimest art
  Appears in this fine color-symphony.

There are deep meanings in these changing moods
  Of wave and sky, that I who reverent stand
Before a flower, and in the strange, old woods
Hear speech too sacred for the common creeds,
Try hard to find, as one who reads and reads
  The words of some great prophet in the land.

O here is living beauty, like the gleam
    In deep, kind eyes when all the soul is there;
This dark-arched bridge whereon I dream and dream,
The lighted shore, the sky, the current free, —
In them is something of humanity,
    Something of God; that makes the scene so fair.

THE WHALING TOWN.

ADZE and hammer and anvil stroke
  Echo not on the shore,
The wharves are crumbling, old, and gray,
  And the whale ships come no more.

Grass grows thick in the empty streets,
  And moss o'er the blackened roofs,
And the people are roused to wonderment
  At the sound of horses' hoofs.

There's not a woman in all the town
  But keeps in memory
The face of a husband, a lover, a friend
  Lost, she says, at sea.

Lost in the days when in every storm
  Some well-known ship went down,
And mothers wept and fathers prayed
  In the little whaling town.

When every sail the children spied
    As they tossed the shining sand,
Came from the storehouse of the sea
    With light for all the land.

And still to the edge of the rotting wharves
    The tides from day to day
Come with an eager wish to bear
    The whaling ships away.

And many an aged mariner looks
    Across the sparkling sea,
And dreams that the waves with sails are flecked
    As of old they used to be.

FLOOD TIDE.

THE tide came up as the sun went down,
    And the river was full to its very brim,
And a little boat crept up to the town
    On the muddy wave, in the morning dim.

But that little boat with its reed-like oar
    Brought news to the town that made it weep
And the people were never so gay as before,
    And they never slept so sound a sleep.

News of a wreck that the boatman had seen
    Off in the bay, in a fierce, wild gale;
Common enough, such things, I ween,
    Yet the women cried and the men were pale.

Strange that a little boat could bring
    Tidings to plunge a town in tears;
Strange how often some small thing
    May shatter and shiver the hope of years.

O, none but the angel with silver wings
    That broods o'er the river and guards the town,
Heeds half of the woe each evening brings,
    As the tide comes up, and the sun goes down.

I WATCH THE SHIPS.

I WATCH the ships by town and lea
   With sails full set glide out to sea,
Till by the distant light-house rock
The breakers beat with roar and shock
And foam fierce flying o'er their decks,
While deep below lie ocean's wrecks;
   What careth she.

I stand beside the beaten quay
And look while laden ships from sea
Come proudly home upon the tide
Like conquering kings at eventide,
Or from fierce fights with wintry gales
Steal shoreward now with tattered sails;
   O cruel sea.

I pass once more the old gray pier
Where men have waited many a year
For ships that ne'er again shall glide
By town and lea on favoring tide,

Strong ships that struggled till the gales
Of winter hid their shrouds and sails
    In ocean drear.

Soft sailing spirits, how they glide
Forth on life's fitful sea untried
To breast the waves and bear the shocks
Beyond the guarded light-house rocks,
To strive and struggle many a year;
Strong souls, indeed, if they can bear
    Life's wind and tide.

I watch beside life's beaten quay
The tides bring back all joyously
To anchor by the sheltered shore
Some freighted full with golden store
From rich spice-fields and perfumed sands
Of soft, luxuriant tropic lands;
    O kindly sea.

But some have met with wintry gales,
And come at last with shattered sails
To anchor by the old, gray pier;

While loving ones in hope and fear
Wait on for some that nevermore
Shall anchor by a peaceful shore;
   O sad, sad sea!

FOUNDRY FIRES.

SEE the foundry fires gleaming
    With a strange and lurid light,
Listen to the anvils ringing
    Measured music on the night;
Clanking, clinking, never shrinking,
    Strike the iron, mould it well!
On the progress of the nations
    Each persistent stroke shall tell.

Showers of fiery sparks are falling
    Thick about the workmen's feet,
Some are carried by the night wind
    Far along the winding street;
Clanking, clinking, never shrinking,
    Labor lifts her arm on high,
And the sparks fly from her anvils
    Out upon the darkened sky.

In the quickened glow of feeling,
    'Neath the anvil strokes of thought,

Ancient errors disappearing,
    Nobler creeds to birth are brought;
Clanking, clinking, never shrinking,
    Strike the truth, yea mould it well!
On the progress of the nations
    Each persistent stroke shall tell.

Crude the mass time's fiery forges
    At your eager feet have hurled,
Centuries of toil must follow
    Ere ye shape a perfect world;
Yet with clanking, clanking, clinking,
    Strike the iron, shape the truth;
Science is indeed beginning,
    Thought is in its lusty youth.

O ye forgemen of the nations,
    Keep the world's great fires alight,
Let the sparks fly from your anvils
    All along the roads of night;
Clanking, clinking, never shrinking,
    Work till stars fade, and the morn
Of a wider faith and knowledge
    In the radiant East is born.

THE OLD NEW ENGLAND MEETING HOUSE.

STANDING alone on the country side,
    Calmly disdaining its walls to hide
Under the garb of vine or tree,
Year after year it frowned at me.

A square-walled church devoid of a spire,
With a lofty gallery for the choir,
Who sang with many an odd inflexion
Hymns from a very old collection.

Many a time I have sat as a child
And listened until my ears were wild
To the basses and tenors with nasal sound,
Through fine old fugue-tunes marching round.

There was a pulpit square and high,
Massively built in days gone by,
With a damask curtain dingy red,
And a winding stair that upward led.

Pews that never were built to please
Prosperous saints who love their ease,
Stood by the aisles with sides so tall
The children could hardly see at all.

Silently down in the old square pews,
As the thirsty earth waits heaven's dews,
The people sat, while the preacher hurled
Righteous wrath at the wicked world;

Or from the words of Jesus read
Gentler things, and softly said
"Now let us pray," so closed his eyes
And lifted his face toward the skies.

To the test of a pulseless plan he brought
Every phase of modern thought,
Nor dreamed that his Calvinistic creed
Was not as wide as human need.

Some in the church, he knew them well,
Were far on the downward way to hell;
They listened like saints and dead to fear,
Sat through the sermons year by year.

But some by the barren service there
He knew were moved to faith and prayer,
On heavenly hopes their hunger fed
And their hearts were always comforted.

The preacher safe in his home on high,
The day of the church at length went by;
The younger people watched it fall,
Gallery, pulpit, pews, and all,

With hardly a thought. Perhaps their creed
Had somewhat changed, since they felt the need
Of buttress and arch and spire and bell
As aids to rescue souls from hell.

I pass by the place, but all is new;
I close my eyes, and there in view
Stands once more on the country side
The strange old church in all the pride

Of its barren walls and pulpit high;
And I think how soon shall all go by
Customs and creeds that have no fear
That a judgment day for them is near.

AT GRANDMOTHER'S.

UNDER the shade of the poplars still,
    Lilacs and locusts in clumps between,
Roses over the window sill,
    Is the dear old house, with its door of green.

Never were seen such spotless floors,
    Never such shining rows of tin,
While the rose-leaf odors that came thro' the doors,
    Told of the peaceful life within.

Here is the room where the children slept,
    Grandmother's children tired with play,
And the famous drawer where the cakes were kept,
    Shrewsbury cookies, and caraway.

The garden walks where the children ran
    To smell the flowers and learn their names,
The children thought, since the world began
    Were never such garden walks for games.

There were tulips and asters in regular lines,
  Sweet-williams and marigolds on their stalks,
Bachelors' buttons and sweet-pea vines,
  And box that bordered the narrow walks.

Pure white lilies stood cornerwise
  From sunflowers yellow and poppies red,
And the summer pinks looked up in surprise
  At the kingly hollyhocks overhead.

Morning glories and larkspur stood
  Close to the neighborly daffodil;
Cabbage roses and southernwood
  Roamed thro' the beds at their own sweet will.

Many a year has passed since then,
  Grandmother's house is empty and still,
Grandmother's babies have grown to men,
  And the roses grow wild o'er the window-sill.

Never again shall the children meet
  Under the poplars gray and tall,
Never again shall the careless feet
  Dance thro' the rose-leaf scented hall.

Grandmother's welcome is heard no more,
    And the children are scattered far and wide,
And the world is a larger place than of yore,
    But hallowed memories still abide.

And the children are better men to-day
    For the cakes and rose-leaves and garden walks,
And grandmother's welcome so far away,
    And the old sweet-williams on their stalks.

CHILDREN OF THE SUN.

A SUNFLOWER tall by the garden wall
    Scornfully nodded his head
To a brilliant poppy whose cheeks below
Were all aflame with a crimson glow.

"I am the child of the sun," he smiled,
    "His color is mine, you see;
Yellow am I to my outmost rim,
While you—how little you look like him."

But the poppy gay still blushing away,
    (And laughing a little too,)
Quietly answered "The sun has told
Me to be red, and you to be gold.

"The morning's hush, and the poppy's blush
    Are dear to the heart of day
As the noontide hour with its triumphs won,
And the flower that rivals the glowing sun.

" Heaven is large, and its chiefest charge
   Is that life shall be broad and free,
And it bids the children of sun and storm
Ne'er to a single type conform."

The sunflower wise looked down in surprise
   At the bold little flower below,
But he learned a lesson there and then
That needs to be learned by many men.

FAIRY-FOLK.

TIME in its mysterious flight
    Circles many a common thing
With a mystic wreath of light,
    All its earth-stains shadowing.

In the dimness of the past
    Human faces grow divine,
The soft shadows deepening fast
    Into living shapes combine.

From the darkness men advance,
    All their common speech enlarged
Into sacred utterance
    With portentous meaning charged.

From the hush of buried years,
    From the silent ages flown,
Every voice that greets our ears
    Has a strange, prophetic tone.

Backward to her legend-lore
   Time with fixed forefinger points,
And the fairy-tales of yore
   With the oil of truth anoints;

Bids us think her ages old
   Swarmed with shapes no longer seen,
Nymphs and gnomes of wood and wold,
   Fauns and fairies on the green.

Dull indeed the world would be
   Must we search the grottoed plain,
Dusky wood, or caverned sea
   For these shadowy friends in vain.

O ye godlike shapes of men,
   Sprites of grove, and sea, and shore,
Mossy meadow, field, and fen,
   Live with us forevermore.

Though to science ye are strange,
   Born of faith and mystery,
Though ye must no longer range
   Fields of sober history,

Still ye sylphs of ages old,
    Spirits of the woods and storms,
Elves and ogres, shy and bold,
    Dreadful dragons, fairy forms,

In our days of childish glee
    Hold high carnival and reign;
Weave the web of dreams and be
    Ministers to later pain.

THE STREET ORGAN.

AN organ grinding below in the street,
   You smile that I think the music sweet,
And you think it strange that I love to listen,
And stranger still that tear-drops glisten
   In my eyes where so seldom a tear is seen.

Ah, if you knew how many things,
Like twilight birds with silver wings,
Came back with these simple airs to me
Over the leagues of summer sea
   My boyhood self and me between,

If you knew that a voice I am hungry to hear
Spoke thro' this music, plaintive, clear,
That a face appeared as the old tunes play,
A face I have longed for night and day
   And never see except in my dreams,

You would not wonder I stop and listen,
You would not wonder tear-drops glisten
In my eyes, as down to the street below,
A few poor pennies I gently throw
   For the grinder to snatch from the passing teams.

THE ANGEL SLEEP.

WHEN the day is done and the shadows fall
    Over the earth like a dusky pall
Then from the unknown, silent deep
Rises the beautiful Angel Sleep.

Over forest and field he spreads his wings
Where the cricket chirps and the wood-bird sings,
And the murmur of voices dies away
Hushed by the Angel calm and gray.

The passions of men that surge and swell,
Are silenced soon 'neath the mystic spell,
And tired hearts long used to weep
Yield to the power of the Angel Sleep.

Softly he broods till the day is come,
Then to his shadows flieth home,
And the spell is gone and the world again
Takes up its burden of care and pain.

THE ANGEL SLEEP.

We call him death, 'tis the Angel Sleep
That comes at last from the silent deep,
And smooths forever the brow of care,
And calms the fever of passion there.

So, we sleep and rest till the morning gray
Breaks once more, of an endless day,
And into the dark, mysterious deep
Flies forever the Angel Sleep.

THE ROOTS OF THE ROSES.

THE roses come and the roses go
But the roots of the roses live under the snow,
Silent their slumber, dreamless, deep,
But by and by they shall wake from sleep.

Our pleasures come and our pleasures go,
But the roots of true joy are hid under the snow,
The hope of the heart has its Winter drear,
But the roses come back in the Spring of the year.

Friendships are born and friendships die,
But love lasts on, tho' the streams be dry,
Her beautiful roses may come and go,
But the roots of the roses live under the snow.

The roses come and the roses go,
But the roots of the roses sleep under the snow,
They are blooming no longer our paths beside,
But their fragrance shall greet us at Eastertide.

CHANCE MEETINGS.

A STRANGER in the moving throng
    To whom I said a careless word
About the weather, or some song,
    Or singer, he and I had heard.

His answer I have wholly lost
    In separate ways we left the place,
But I keep what I value most,
    The memory of a human face.

And still I feel within my heart
    The thrill his touch awakened there,
As, clasping hands, we moved apart,
    Each ignorant of the other's sphere.

We are not strangers, you and I,
    Who touch but once each other's hands,
Amidst the throng whose interests lie
    In many spheres, in many lands.

The quick, responsive, friendly clasp
    Of hands, the smile our faces wear,
Have genuine meanings each may grasp,
    They tell the common life we bear.

No matter where, by chance we met,
    The thought is free of time or place,
I keep what I can ne'er forget—
    The memory of a human face.

THE POET PASSED MY WAY.

[Written for the tribute to John G. Whittier on his eightieth birthday.]

THE poet passed my way
   Bearing great handfuls of fair flowers,
Pure white with golden gay,
   Plucked from his soul's tilled garden plots and bowers.

They are but common blooms,
   Fragrant, yet fading like the rest;
Enough to deck my rooms
   I'll gather, said I, following toward the West.

But in a moment more,
   Stooping to lift them from the sod,
I found the poet bore,
   Not flowers, but great thoughts rooted deep in God.

THE VOYAGE OF SLEEP.

To sleep I give myself away,
    Unclasp the fetters of the mind,
Forget the sorrows of the day,
    The burdens of the heart unbind.

With empty sail this tired bark
    Drifts out upon the sea of rest,
While all the shore behind grows dark
    And silence reigns from east to west.

At last awakes the hidden breeze
    That bears me to the land of dreams,
Where music sighs among the trees,
    And murmurs in the winding streams.

O weary day, O weary day,
    That dawns in fear and ends in strife,
That brings no cooling draught to allay
    The burning fever-thirst of life.

THE VOYAGE OF SLEEP.

O sacred night when angel hands
    Are pressed upon the tired brow,
And when the soul on shining sands
    Descends with angels from the prow.

To sleep I give myself away,
    My heart forgets its vague unrest,
And all the clamor of the day,
    And drifts toward the quiet west.

GEMS THAT ARE RAREST.

GEMS that are rarest
   Hide in the sea,
Flowers that are fairest
   Plucked not may be;

Sunshine the brightest
   Comes after rain,
Hearts that seem lightest
   Know bitterest pain.

Truth deepest lying
   Wakes to thy view
When, self-denying,
   To self thou'rt true.

Heaven is nearest
   When thou, sin-tossed,
Gloomily fearest
   Thy soul is lost.

LA DOULEUR DU PEINTRE.

THERE is crape on the studio door
    And none pass in to-day,
And the sunlight on the floor
    Falls cold and gray;
And the painter's head on his hands is bent
In a new and strange bewilderment.

He has brought a flower of gold,
    The daffodil of her France,
It lies in her fingers cold,
    A glittering lance;
And he lives once more, with her alone,
The sunny life of Barbizon.

Together they climb the hill
    And stand in the sunset glow
And watch while the breezes fill
    The sails below;
And she bids him compass with his art
The beautiful things of eye and heart.

So there come from his willing hand
    Results more swift and true,
As the harvest ears expand
    In sun and dew;
And her love makes radiant all his life
And he blesses God for the gift of his wife.

But sorrow stands by the shrine
    In the darkest place of his soul,
And bids him drink the wine
    In her silver bowl;
And his nerves are wrought with subtle pain,
And he bows his head in grief again.

Strange that we never know
    Our own till they are dead;
That life's best harvests grow
    When life is fled;
That love comes not to its second birth
Till our lips have echoed " Earth to earth."

Crape on the studio door,
    A cheerless light within,

LA DOULEUR DU PEINTRE.

  A heart that shall never more
   Know care or sin;
And a hand that lifts not whence it fell
The brush it was used to wield so well.

SOMETIME.

SOMETIME, sometime,
    The clouds of ignorance shall part asunder,
And we shall see the fair, blue sky of truth
Spangled with stars, and look with joy and wonder
    Up to the happy dream-lands of our youth,
        Where we may climb.

Sometime, sometime,
The passion of the heart we keep dissembling
    Shall free herself, and rise on silver wing,
And all these broken chords of music, trembling
    Deep in the soul, our lips shall learn to sing,
        A strain sublime.

Sometime, sometime,
Love's broken links shall all be reunited,
    But not upon the ashy forge of pain;
The full-blown roses dead, the sweet buds blighted
    Shall bloom beside life's garden walks again,
        In fairer clime.

Sometime, sometime,
The prophet's unsealed lips shall straight deliver
　　The message of eternal life uncursed;
Wind-swept, the poet's heaven-tuned soul shall quiver,
　　And from his trembling lyre at length shall burst
Immortal rhyme.

'TWERE BETTER TO LOVE.

*" 'Tis better to have loved and lost
Than never to have loved at all."*

'TWERE better to love, though the heart be broken,
  Than to sit alone from passion free,
Never to have a sign or token
  Of the life that deepest lies in thee.

' Twere better to love, though peace should never
  Softly climb to thy soul again,
Than to live the blinded life forever
  Of barren-hearted, loveless men.

' Twere better far that the gates, in shadow,
  Of heaven, should once have come in view
Than that thou till death, from thy dull meadow,
  Shouldst never have seen the pearl and blue.

THE HEARTH IS COLD.

THE hearth is cold, the fire no more
    Glows in the twilight gray,
'Tis colder, colder than before
    The soft flame had its way.

Love's fire is quenched, its glow is o'er,
    Its ashes now are gray;
My heart is colder than before
    The glad flame had its way.

I shall forget it more and more,
    This passion of a day,
Yet I am glad though it is o'er
    The fire *once* had its way.

AFTER SEPARATION.

YOU are here, O my love, at my side
    And I struggle to keep
My starved spirit from reeling
In the tumult and toss of the tide
    That sweeps in from the unsounded, deep,
Shoreless ocean of feeling.

The time has been long, dearest heart,
    But a moment of this
Would make balance for ages;
It were kind to keep lovers apart,
    If, at meeting, God give them such bliss
As comes now for our wages.

I am learning the meaning at last
    Of the speech of my kind,
Often heard, little heeded;
Press your lips to my lips, hold me fast,
    O my love; I was sick, I was blind;
Heaven knew what I needed.

I PLUCKED A DAISY.

I PLUCKED a daisy by the walk,
   A white field daisy, carelessly,
I saw it tremble on its stalk
   And cast a piteous glance at me.

Its sisters seemed to chide me too,
   As if I had destroyed a life
That God had given some work to do,
   In earth's wild garden lands of strife.

And nodding all their golden heads,
   Encased in bonnets snowy white,
Tears seemed to fall in crystal beads
   From their soft eyes, that summer night.

O little daisies of the sod,
   One law controls your life and mine,
Ye are the humblest flowers of God,
   But ye like man are half divine.

And as ye cheer the dusty walk
    And whiten all the meadows fair,
I see a spirit on each stalk
    That trembles in the dewy air.

Bloom on in simple faith and joy
    In purity and tenderness,
I will not needlessly destroy
    Your golden heads and snowy dress.

THE MEADOW LANDS.

THE tide flows in and out and leaves
   Its richness on the meadow lands,
The furrowed surface-soil upheaves,
   And sprinkles life among the sands.

Across the meadow lands of life
   The tide of time flows and recedes,
Its muddy wave brings woe and strife,
   But forms the soil for noble deeds.

The tide flows in and out and brings
   New beauty to the meadow lands,
With lavish tenderness it flings
   Fair flowers across the silver sands.

SMALL AND GREAT.

THE ripp'e that stirs on the sea of thought,
   As we drop our smallest question there,
Into the ocean's life is wrought
   And moves it everywhere.

Who strikes a chord in the human soul,
   Be he laborer, poet, priest, or sage,
Makes music that rings from pole to pole
   And lasts from age to age.

The feeblest prayer that to heaven flies
   Has the infinite power in its wing
And the treasure of peace it brings from the skies
   Is not a foreign thing.

For all is in each, and each in all,
   All is human and all divine,
The small is the great, the great the small,
   And truth is mine and thine.

LIFE.

A GOLDEN gleam between the past and present,
    A feeble, flickering, unearthly flame;
A light that flashes up amidst the darkness
    And fades again as quickly as it came.

A wave that rises noiseless from the ocean
    And breaks with soft, sad moaning on the shore;
A white-capped wave that lifts its crest to heaven
    And sinks into the silent deep once more.

A sudden, startled strain that strikes at evening
    Through all the slumbering air from hill to hill;
A strange child-song of mingled mirth and madness
    That wakes a wayward echo, and is still.

A silver-sheeted spectre-form that wanders
    On some mysterious shore at dead of night,
A moment weeps its woes, then wingless rises
    Into the chambers of the infinite.

IT MATTERS MUCH.

WHETHER I live in the crowded town
    Or in open lands beside the sea,
So long as I live for love's sweet crown
    What difference can it make to me;
But whether I feel the trembling touch
    Of the hand of need where'er it be,
        This matters much.

Whether the winds of fortune blow
    Over my head with soft caress,
What difference, if I may but know
    I am healing some sad heart's distress;
But whether I feel the woe of such
    As long for a brother's tenderness,
        This matters much.

For life with its suffering and sin
    Hath little to give of peace or rest,
And I know the care that hideth in

Many and many a tender breast;
So I pray that God through my hand's touch
May heal some hearts by grief opprest,
This matters much.

NOT IN VAIN.

No matter how relentlessly
    The storm sweeps o'er the night,
Life is not lived in vain if we
    But anchor to the right.

Life is not lived in vain although
    Our fairest hopes decay,
And ere we die the lichens grow
    Over their ruins gray.

Life is not lived in vain if we,
    Amidst the winter's gloom,
May clothe one barren, leafless tree
    With fragrant summer bloom.

If we may call the stars again
    Into some darkened sky
It cannot be that life is vain
    Although its dreams go by.

For he whose life was most divine
    Had only this success:
To cause a few hope-rays to shine
    Amidst earth's hopelessness,

TO A DOUBTER.

I CANNOT say " Believe " to thee
   Whose lips from thought's clear springs have drunk,
   The questions of the age have sunk
Deep in thy quivering soul, I see.

For I should hear thee rightly say,
   " Whate'er is true, thy well-turned speech
   Doth not the mind's recesses reach
Nor light the spirit's hidden way."

Thy soul for certainty is sick,
   While they who wrangle over forms,
   Untroubled by faith's fiercer storms
Feed well on sweets of rhetoric.

I see thee like a long caged bird,
   Thou beat'st thy bars with broken wing,
   And flutter'st, feebly echoing
The far-off music thou hast heard.

TO A DOUBTER.

Oblivion tempts thee, yet be wise,
   Walk on awhile in storm and shade,
   These ghosts that haunt thy feet may fade;
Thought hath its cock-crow and sunrise.

Perhaps the unseen plan shall prove
   More than thy noblest longings crave;
   Thy life may sweep beyond the grave
Into a universe of love,

Where doubt may cease, wrong turn to right,
   God's diverse ways be reconciled,
   And thou so long His orphan child
Meet Him upon the hills of light.

THE SUICIDE.

HIS heart was breaking, breaking,
    'Neath loads of care and wrong;
Who blames the man for taking
    What life denied so long?

She promised rest and gladness;
    She mocked him o'er and o'er;
She bathed with seas of sadness
    His spirit's island shore.

She bade him lightness borrow
    Beneath her trees of yew,
Though all the dreadful sorrow
    Of the dark world he knew.

He had no mind to flatter
    An age with falsehood drest;
She hated him; no matter,
    The man is now at rest.

He begged for light from heaven,
    No light his soul could see;
He snatched what was not given;
    He sleeps, now let him be.

His heart was breaking, breaking
    'Neath loads of care and wrong;
Heaven must not blame his taking
    What she denied so long.

AN ANSWER.

" A God, a God their severance ruled."

YOU tell me that all can be strong and wise,
    That men can choose their fate;—
This is one of your winning lies,
    It comes to me too late.

A favored few to the purple born
    Laugh at the threats of chance;
Look at the race, oppressed and worn,
    Poor slaves of circumstance.

We may take what we will from life, you say,
    The whitest bread, or a stone;
We may walk on the sunniest side of the way,
    Or sit in the shade alone.

Bread to the hungriest denied,
    Love to the lover's heart,
Fields uncut at the harvest-tide,
    And reapers, kept apart;

I pray you look o'er the walls of your creed,
   (*Heaven-builded* though they be,)
At the shackled shapes of human need,
   Of pain and misery.

What we are given we have, and fate
   (Name it God if you will) may be kind
In it all, but she shuts the iron gate
   Of her plan, and keeps us blind.

And, in the future who can tell,
   If life still be not lost,
Whether we hug the harbor well,
   Or on strange seas are tossed.

Pause by these silent, salt-waved seas
   That stretch to worlds unseen;
Blows to thee here on the landward breeze
   A breath from forests green?

Then, hope for the best, and pray and pray,
   Since unseen powers there be,
But do not think that the world to-day
   Wants cheap philosophy.

DESPONDENCY.

Let the age its discords shrill
    Madly shriek from hill to hill;
" *Thou* art tired, best be still."

Dost thou think its wrongs to right,
Wilt thou try to cure its spite?
Tears shall quickly blind thy sight.

Stronger hands than thine have failed,
Braver hearts than thine have quailed,
By its weapons coarse assailed.

Pharisees in Church and state
Sit in plenty at its gate;
Prophets do but rouse its hate.

Custom is the Church's god,
Greed walks openly abroad;
Truth sits weeping on the sod.

Let the age its discords shrill
    Madly shriek from hill to hill;
    Thou art powerless, be still.

A FIRE OF STRAW.

A FIRE of straw in field or town
   Obscures the bluest skies,
To-day's complaining echoes drown
   Time's grandest harmonies.

One trifling error on the page
   All satisfaction mars;
So earth's stray swamp-lights more engage
   The mind than heaven's stars.

Man's deepest instincts bid him rise
   Among the rose-red spheres;
But some old custom, when he tries,
   Enchains him fast with fears.

O empty, phosphorescent gleam,
   Swift-fading fire of straw,
When ye are gone, still lives my dream
   Of worlds of love and law.

REABSORPTION INTO DEITY.

"Having obtained tranquillity one is not troubled; and remaining in it, even at the time of death, he passes on to extinction in the Supreme Spirit."—*Bhagavad Gita.*

WITH undimmed eye
    I listen to the wisdom old which saith
Man shall be reabsorbed in God at death;
The human spirit is a deep-drawn breath
    Of Him on high.

    No living thing
Save man, has ever dreamed of higher spheres
Wherein to taste delights the fleeting years
Have here denied, or balance this world's fears
    And suffering.

    Sad hearts that pray,
Soft petaled, crimson flowers that bloom and fade,
Trees that grow sturdier in storm and shade,
Begotten are they all of God, not made
    Like cups of clay.

REABSORPTION INTO DEITY.

      Why have we right
To some chief boon of immortality
Not given our brothers of the wood and sky:
Strong beasts, soft-fluttering, winged birds that fly
      From light to light?

      Then let me go
Into the great hereafter joyously,
To live, yet not to live apart from thee;
From thy great life the life now lent to me
      No more to flow.

      The Ocean vast
Has need of all his wayward waves and streams,
The Central Sun has need of all his beams;
It is full time these strange, fantastic dreams
      Of mine were past.

      I turn to thee,
O thou great Father, Universal Soul,
Unheeding nature's myriad bells that toll
Dead things; since all life's rivers roll
      Back to their sea.

Ah, what can be
So grand for nature or for man, what fate
So lofty, as to sweep in solemn state
At evening, back through a wide open gate
    To Deity!

EDER'S WATCHTOWER.

I LOVE the soft incoming tide
   That breaks in showers of silver spray,
I love the dawn that opens wide
   The floodgates of the living day,

I love the harvest voice that speaks
   From each green blade of growing corn,
I love the first fair beam that breaks
   Across the heart in sorrow's morn;

But fairer than the silver tide,
   And brighter than the morning's flood
The light on Bethlehem's meadows wide
   Where Eder's ancient watchtower stood.

O little town of Bethlehem,
   Where Christ, the perfect man, was born,
Thy memories are dear to them
   Whose earth-shod feet are travel-worn.

The Angels' song thy shepherds heard
   Is echoing along the years,
Thou hast an ever welcome word
   For human woes and human fears;

O fairer than the silver tide
   And brighter than the morning's flood
The light across thy meadows wide,
   Where Eder's ancient watchtower stood.

The plains of life are cold and gray
   Like those beneath the Syrian stars,
Our lips are dumb when we would pray,
   Our hopes are all defaced with scars,

The promise of a perfect world
   So faintly gleams on distant hills
That faith from her strong tower is hurled,
   And wild despair her bosom fills;

But thou, dear town of Bethlehem,
   Dost promise to our darkened race
That heaven's fairest diadem
   The forehead of mankind shall grace.

And we are glad, this Christmas time,
    That first upon thy starlit hills,
Where purple Syrian harebells climb,
    And drink the freshness of the rills,

There shone the sacred Christmas light,
    And echoed clear the Angels' song,
That still rings out upon the night
    Of human misery and wrong.

O fairer than the silver tide,
    And brighter than the morning's flood
The light on Bethlehem's meadows wide,
    Where Eder's ancient watchtower stood.

DAY OF THE TRIUMPHANT SUN.

IT is the ancient Yule-tide,
    The time of mirth and cheer;
With memories gay, upon his way
    We'll send the good, old year.
We'll deck him out with garlands
    Of wild vines from the rocks,
With holly red, we'll wreathe his head
    And bind his silver locks.

At Yule our Norse forefathers
    Built high their sacred fires,
And in the glow hung mistletoe
    About their homes and byres;
And we their loyal children
    Ere yet the year is done,
This Christmas day will own the sway
    Of "the triumphant Sun."

At Yule the goddess Berchta,
    When shining Fagrahvel

His golden car had driven far
   The Spring's approach to tell,
Walked through the frozen furrows
   And sprinkled gladness there,
While corn and wheat sprang 'neath her feet
   Upon the meadows bare.

And Odin the creator,
   His fiery horse astride,
O'er land and sea rode wild and free
   To check the Winter-tide;
And fountains from their prisons
   With merry songs burst forth,
And warriors gay appeared, to slay
   The giant of the North.

At Yule we deck our houses
   With wreaths of evergreen,
And peace and joy without alloy
   On every face are seen;
The Yule-tide fires are lighted
   And Yule-tide carols sung,
And, loud and low, across the snow
   The sweet church chimes are rung.

And Christian texts are mingled
    With holly berries red
As through the land, from hand to hand,
    Fair Christmas gifts are spread.
For Christian memories hoary
    With Norse dwell side by side,
And Yule wears now upon her brow
    The crown of Christmas-tide.

MY PUREST LONGINGS SPRING.

My purest longings spring
   From the divine,
The sweetest songs I sing
   They are not mine.

I chisel the rude stone
   With trembling hand,
The statue comes alone
   At God's command.

Beyond earth's tainted air
   I sometimes fly
On wings of faith and prayer;
   Yet 'tis not I.

Not I but He who lights
   My flickering creeds;
The Power that unites
   My broken deeds.

Not I but God; for He,
My larger life,
Fulfils Himself in me
With ceaseless strife.

BROTHERHOOD.

THERE'S little to choose in this world of ours
    'Twixt the peasant and the King,
Tho' the monarch feasts with wine and flowers,
    And wears a goodly ring,
While the peasant sports on the village green
    In a suit of homespun gray;
The pleasure of one is just as keen
    As the other's, every way.

Each carries a heart that sings and sighs,
    By turns, as the changes come;
Each finds in life some sad surprise,
    At which his lips grow dumb.
Passion and pride and lust and greed
    Are mixed with the good in each,
And deep in his soul is the human need
    That Heaven alone can reach.

The monarch has laws he must obey
    And burdens he must bear,

He envies the peasant, many a day,
   His lack of kingly care;
And both look into the same fair sky,
   Fenced with its golden stars,
And wonder what vast treasures lie
   Behind those glittering bars.

THE ANCIENT GODS ARE DEAD.

THE ancient gods are dead!
    Jove rules no longer o'er the Olympian plain,
Old ocean waits for Neptune's car in vain,
Apollo tunes no more his golden lyre,
Vesuvius trembles not with Vulcan's fire,
Mars leads not now the armies of the world,
Young Cupid's darts at Pluto are not hurled,
    And Venus' charms are fled.

    The ancient gods are dead!
Valhalla's noble halls are empty now,
Where Thor, the mighty thunderer, from his brow
Shot lightnings forth upon the trembling earth,
And Odin held his wassail, and loud mirth
Echoed from roof to roof, as went the feast,
Until the day dawned and the waiting east
    Made radiant Baldur's head.

    The ancient gods are dead!
On Sinai's rugged heights the clouds appear,

The prophet goes no longer there to hear
The eternal word, nor full of gladness sees
Heaven's judgments break on all his enemies.
The flower-sprinkled sod at God's command
Reeks not with useless blood, nor thro' the land
     His vengeful armies spread.

     The ancient gods are dead!
No Roman despot sits on heaven's throne
Dispensing judgments by his will alone;
Bids some ascend to heaven, some sink to hell,
In arbitrary bliss or woe to dwell.
The true God asks no sacrifice of blood,
Nor nails His victims to the cruel wood
     In others' guilty stead.

     The ancient gods are dead!
Law rules majestic in the courts above,
And has no moods, but hand in hand with love,
Sweeps thro' the universe, and smiling sees
The spheres obedient to her vast decrees.
Proclaims all men, not slaves, but sons of God,
And breathes the message of His Fatherhood;
     The true God is not dead.

O EASTER QUEEN.

O EASTER, queen of all the days
   That wear the Church's crown,
Upon our troubled human ways
   Thy calm, fair face looks down.

Thou cam'st this morning thro' the fields
   And spoke some magic word,
And all the plain where harvest yields
   With pulsing life was stirred.

The jacqueminot and tulip gay
   About thy pathway pressed,
But golden-petaled lilies lay
   In triumph on thy breast.

The messenger of death bowed low
   To kiss thy conquering feet,
Life, trembling, seemed at last to know
   Her victory complete.

Thou camest to the sleeping town
   And where the mourner lay,

And joy rose from her prison brown
    And rolled the stone away.

Thou hast the urn whose spices blend
    To sweeten all the year;
O Easter queen, new courage send
    To us who worship here.

O Easter, queen of all the days
    That wear the Church's crown,
To form thy purest aureole-rays,
    Heaven sends its sunlight down.

FOUNTAINS ABBEY.

I NEVER knew so well how throbbed the heart
  Of those old centuries we keep apart
So eagerly from ours, as when I stood
Alone, one Autumn day, in softest mood
Beside the ruins England loves so well,
Her Fountains Abbey in the vale of Skell.

A sea of living meadow far and near
Laughed at the menace of the waning year;
But like some lonely rock far up the shore,
That ne'er again shall hear the plash of oar
Nor feel the tides, apart from field and wood
These ruined walls and broken cloisters stood.

Univied pillars here and there aloof,
That once had borne the weight of gilded roof,
And gothic arch, and heaven-lifted tower,
Disdained the threats of time and all its power,
And seemed like hoary men who bid us try
The courtlier manners of an age gone by.

By ancient buttressed walls I still could trace
The Abbey's separate parts, could, keep in place
On this side and on that the foaming Skell,
Nave, chancel, chapter house, and crypt and cell;
A living harmony of chiselled stone,
A gothic forest in this valley grown.

It was not strange I felt once more the thrill
Of the old life, for every place at will
Brings back its myriad dead, not ghosts but men,
Who take their old tasks up, and walk again
The common ways. Alive grew plain and wood
With the white robed Cistercian brotherhood.

Some tilled the fields, some from the forest came
Laden with fresh cut fuel or with game;
Some tended glowing ovens deep and wide,
Or turned the juicy spit from side to side.
Some thoughtful, with the air of high bred men,
Cowls back, sat silent, wielding brush or pen.

In holy sanctuary, where the east
Poured mellow splendors thro' the church, a priest
With broidered robes at the high altar sung

A noble mass whose echoes faintly rung
Into the raftered gloom and lingered there,
Like Skell's own murmurs on the evening air.

On traceried windows rich with red and gold,
Time honored legends of the Church were told;
Martyrs and saints, children of want and fear,
Had reached an aureoled existence here.
In jewelled splendor, over all, was he
Of Bethlehem's manger and Gethsemane.

I saw the abbot like a potentate
Come riding proudly thro' the open gate,
While, as he rode, a cowled monastic bore
With lifted hands, a silver cross before;
And every tonsured brother, low or high,
Made reverent gesture as his lord went by.

I saw the weary traveller alight
Before the abbey walls at dead of night,
Too tired to take the bridle from his steed,
Too tired to tell the answering monk his need,
Or claim the hospitality here given
Like Israel's manna or the dew of heaven.

The castellated feudal towers that frowned
Their moated terrors on the country round,
And o'er the serf-tilled soil with verdure drest,
Proclaimed a sullen sway from east to west,
From neighboring woods looked on, amazed to see
Such peace, such open hospitality.

O golden days, I said, when rich and poor,
Knights riding home across the lonely moor,
The humblest laborer in field or fen,
Princes and cassocked priests and serving men
Were ever welcome to an abbey's fires,
Its ripening fruits, the fat kine in its byres.

O wondrous age, when poets sang their songs
In these cool cells, unhindered by the throngs
That love not melody.   When Science knew
A place where, welcome, she might search the blue,
Still dome of heaven, or unsuspected pry
Amidst the rocks, her field the earth and sky.

O happy men, whom cruel, cureless hate,
Love unrequited, festering sores of state,
The din of clashing creeds, domestic strife,

The lusts and lies that sicken us of life,
Drove here for shelter. Discords as of hell
Were hushed within you here beside the Skell.

O happy, happy age, too wise to hurl
The soul forever back into the whirl
Of tempted life. To bid the tired brain
Keep ever listening the one refrain
That maddened most. Too wise to let men waste
All noblest energy in fever haste.

O ruined abbey, all the hope and fear
Of all the centuries are gathered here,
Devotion, brotherhood, and lust and greed,
Man's noblest triumph, and his darkest deed.
The great world's soul is in these violet blooms
Above your nameless monks' forgotten tombs.

TO LORD HAMILTON OF DALZELL.

ETCHED clear against September skies
    Upon the lowland landscape rise
The rugged towers of Dalzell.

A stately castle by the Clyde,
With parks that stretch on every side,
And lime-lined avenues, the pride
    Of all the sons of Motherwell;

In earlier times, with moat and keep,
A feudal fortress, stern and steep,
    It frowned upon the neighboring woods,

And challenged hostile chiefs to try
Their strength, and watched with jealous eye
Cowled monks on stately steeds ride by,
    And knights with helmets 'neath their hoods.

But now it has no frown, no fear,
Its owner is a genial peer,
    Of soldier sires a soldier son,—

From whose dark-panelled walls look down
Brave men who gained a just renown,
Fair women fit for any crown—
   By double right a Hamilton.

A liberal mind and liberal heart
Are his, how often kept apart
   In nobles as in humbler men,

A thoughtful man who scans the page
Of history to know his age,
And to the strife of work and wage,
   Not all unmoved, turns back again.

On Scottish soil from sea to sea,
Though many castles fair there be,
   I know not one that blends so well

Old types and new. And all the place
Seems haunted by the perfect grace
Of Lady Emily's sweet face,
   The dear, dead mistress of Dalzell.

Since England's future king and queen
Have lately passed her gates between,
   A royal charm Dalzell has won;

Yet here within her ivied walls,
Her old-world chambers, spacious halls
A subtler charm my heart enthralls.

Within me flame ancestral fires,
Here wakes the blood of all my sires
   Of the proud race of Hamilton.

The scutcheoned panels overhead
Recall my ancestors, not dead
   To me, though ruined abbeys keep

Their mouldering dust, and castles gray
That once were theirs, to proud decay
Are fallen, and time has wiped away
   The fond inscriptions where they sleep.

My Lord, thy hospitality
I would repay, would welcome thee
   Across the ocean where I dwell.

And may I not some day return,
When Autumn from her golden urn
Hath dropped red fires on brae and burn,
   To thy fair towers of Dalzell?

So shalt thou still increase my claim
(Though mine is an untitled name)
   To pride in all that thou hast done,

And make me prouder still to share
With thee the blood that she who bare
Me gave. And prouder still to wear
   The ancient name of Hamilton.

SONNETS.

O RESTLESS POET SOUL.

O RESTLESS poet soul that know'st no bounds,
    A world of unspent song lies back of thee;
  Thou livest in a land of melody
For thee earth has no common sights or sounds.

With wool the people bid thee stuff thine ears;
    " Be satisfied," they cry, " with what we teach;"
  Then laugh, and say: " What is it that he hears ?
    Song is but song, truth loves staid forms of speech."

But thou, with music melting thee to tears,
    Bring'st nobler strains through their fond, fragile creeds,
  Like one who pipes sweet songs on simple reeds;
And thou art deaf to all their frets and fears.

Sing then thy strains however poor they be,
A world of unspent song lies back of thee.

THE AWAKENING.

TOO long my soul has lain in sordid sleep
   Floating on seas whose depths I never knew,
At last, aroused, I look into the deep
   In wonder, all is old, yet, O so new.

Love, love, sweet love, what gift is thine to show
   The soul life's inmost depths, what power
To make the hidden currents seen that flow
   From root to root, from stem to leaf and flower.

O, I am now more human with my kind,
   More reverent, no longer in the sod
The home of souls, man's final rest, I find,
   For my dim eyes behold his source, the God

Of whom no sage on earth, no saint above
Can say a greater thing than *He is love*.

LOVE'S SLAVERY.

ON the low levels of my love for thee
    I talk of its pure passion as of *chains*
That bind my soul in gold-linked slavery,
    A willing bondage, yet not free from pains.

But when love once has reached the hill-tops, high
    Above the murky sphere where " mine and thine "
Hold feud forever, all in vain I try
    To find betwixt our souls a bounding line

I would not be thy slave, though servitude
    To thee exceed rule of another's heart,
Bonds chafe, chains clank, and in some moment rude
    The servant and his lord perforce may part.

O love, for us the sweet slave life is done,
The perfect *union* of our souls begun.

SEPARATION.

'TIS torture, yet I would not it were less,
   Since anguish is the sure tide-mark of love;
Say thou art glad, dear heart, at my distress,
   Thus should I prove thee if 'twere right to prove.

Yet do I truly love thee, selfish fear
   Is so inwoven with all my thought of thee?
I love, *I* suffer, O that he were here
   That he might say again that he loves *me*.

Or should I be so inly glad to know
   That thou wert suffering, if my love were true;
Would love not rather all its own forego
   Than have the knowledge that thou sufferest too,

O agony of love, does life's best bliss
Bring always with it questioning like this?

PAIN.

I KNEW not pain till I had felt my soul
   Sweep outward on a wide, wild sea of love,
And then had seen the friendly stars above
Fade, one by one, and cold, gray silence roll
Into the heaven where tender thoughts had hung
To light me o'er the silver-crested foam.
"O shivering soul," I cried, "come home, come home,
Night's dews are cold, thy cloak from thee is flung,
He loves thee not, or if he loves, he shares
His heart with other suppliants beside thee;
It is not well in fruitless agony
To spend the hours; betake thee to thy prayers."
Then bruised and blind my soul turned to the land,
But moaned all night upon the yellow sand.

LOVE LETTERS.

WHO keeps not somewhere safely stored away,
    Like jewels in a casket quaint, from view,
  A bundle of love-letters, old or new,
Yellow with age, or fresh as buds of May.

Who, sometimes, in the silence of the night,
    With stealthy fingers does not draw them forth,
    Dear, tender treasures, not of common worth,
And live the old love o'er that suffered blight.

Yes, here are mine, not faded yet with years;
    Sometimes I laugh at the old tender flame
    That kindled them, but is it any shame
To whisper they are wet, to-night, with tears.

What strange, persistent power love has to hold
Its life, though all its ashes have grown cold.

THE VIRGIN'S SHRINE.

WHO kneels in silent rapture on the sod
   In open sky, or on the marble floor
Of some dark church, his soul's true prayers says o'er,
Adores the holy motherhood of God.

The shrine of Mary is not reverenced less
   By men whose feet are swift, whose arms are strong,
   Than by sweet woman souls to whom belong
By right maternity and gentleness.

All lofty things in our conception meet
   In the divine, all beautiful and good;
   The sterner attributes of Fatherhood
Alone make not for man a God complete.

If we at Mary's altars best may feel
God's true maternity, there should we kneel.

IF CHRIST WERE HERE.

IF Christ were with us in this restless age,
    Where light and shade so strangely intermix,
To all the woeful clash of work and wage,
The complex questionings that minds engage,
Men's strifes, could he the meanings true affix?
To any of the sullen, sickening waves
Of doubt and death that cross our social seas
Could he speak peace? From deep-dug, dreamless
    graves,
Where silken-shrouded lie the world's dead slaves,
Could he call back men slain by lust and ease?
O, Master, while we long for thee, and hold
Thy love a mantle where our hearts might fold
Their aches, we fear that even thou shouldst see
The problems of the age too deep for thee.

A DREAM OF CHRIST.

I.

I DREAMED that Christ was here, and, as of old,
  The people cried "Jesus is going by";
And I, knowing his time had come to die,
Made eager move his passing steps to hold.
"In one short hour he will be back," they said,
So, waiting, I began to wonder how
I should receive him, whether I should bow
Low at his feet, nor dare to lift my head,
Or, as a man, with human feeling strong,
Meeting his fellow man, gives him his hand
And says, "Brother," or "Master, I have long
Waited the day before you close to stand;"
I might, at last, unhindered see and feel
The truth about the Christ to whom men kneel.

II.

Decision quick took shape within my mind
To greet the Saviour in a manful way,
To look into his deep, soft eyes and say,
"Master, thou know'st truth is hard to find,
The wisest men are blind and lead the blind;
Tell us hast thou indeed more light than they?
And he, I thought, a man sincere and kind,
Will put aside all strangeness, and obey
My wish, and I, at last, shall know what he
Believes, and what the grounds of his faith are.
So, with a sweet sense of expectancy,
As for my dearest friend, I watched afar
His coming, till at length I woke alone,
And all my hope of finding truth was gone.

DEEPENING THE CHANNEL.

A ROCKY channel from the harbor led
    The ships to sea, a blue but shallow sound
With surging tides, upon whose treacherous bed
    The keels of heavy vessels ground and ground.

The channel must be deepened, men agree,
    And so, great thunderous blasts of rock they blew,
And all the sleepy sands were dredged; till, free
    From fear, the heaviest ships went swiftly through.

We fret and foam, as if our surface tide
    Was fathoms deep, and never know the truth
Till love or sorrow through the water ride,
    And grate its keel upon the sands of youth;

God cleaves the rock beneath the channel blue,
And then his noblest ships sail safely through.

MATTHEW ARNOLD.

AS he who seeks to know the depths that lie
    Beneath his feet with patience gropes his way,
By aid of scarpèd cliff and mountain high
And fossil fragment new to history,
Down to the lowest rocks, once pliant clay,
So thou with thy clear penetrating eye
Hast looked below the surface mind of man,
And, loving truth, hast helped us classify
As Glacial or Silurian, thoughts that lie
In layers deep with little seeming plan.

Yet, too, a poet, far from things like these,
Past ruddy Mars and distant Pleiades,
To thought's high spheres thou lead'st our lagging feet,
Where all the plan of life is shown complete.

ELISHA MULFORD.

I KNEW a man (O that he still were here)
    Who in an age of falsehood cared for truth,
    Who loved the uncorrupt ideals of youth,
And through the shams of later life saw clear.

While others worshipped idols he drew near
    The heart of things, and there into his face
    God looked, and he in God's, till all the grace
'That in the aureoles of saints appear

Seemed thrown, a rich divineness, round his head,
    And light such as the old saints never knew
    Sweept through his mind. The church to thought too dead
To feel the worth of men like him, withdrew

Her sympathy; " He wages not my strife,"
She said. But Truth was richer for his life.

HARVARD COMMENCEMENT.

WHEN Cambridge elms are green, and many an oar
   Beneath the Charles' muddy wave is dipt,
   And Boston spires, Venetian-sunset tipt,
Watch gliding gondolas from shore to shore,

Then doth Fair Harvard open wide her door,
   And speak her annual welcome, magic-lipped,
   To all her sons, of age and honors stripped
Again, boys still at forty or fourscore.

Grave statesmen then drink healths from ruddy bowls,
   And Freshman follies laughingly recall,
   And reverend parsons, sober, spare, and tall,
Relax the tension of their long-strained souls.

O Cambridge elms, O College growing gray,
Guard well the secrets of Commencement-day!

www.ingramcontent.com/pod-product-compliance
Lightning Source LLC
Chambersburg PA
CBHW030316170426
43202CB00009B/1025